Copyright © 2024 Monthly Munchkins
All copyright laws and rights reserved. Published in the U.S.A.

Paperback ISBN: 978-1-63731-901-7
Hardcover ISBN: 978-1-63731-903-1
eBook ISBN: 978-1-63731-902-4

In a town full of fun beneath the sunny skies,
Lived a munchkin named July with twinkling eyes.
He loved to play from morning to night,
For in the warm sun, he laughed with much delight.

His friend June came by with a picnic to share,
Hotdogs, chips, and lemonade made with care.
They sat in the park enjoying the day,
As the sun shone down in its bright, golden way.

July loved the beach with its warm, sandy shore,
He built castles and forts, and then built some more.
With June and August, they splashed in the sea,
The air filled with laughter and they felt carefree!

July loved the month of July, with its holidays bright,
From picnics to fireworks, every day was just right.
The beautiful days made each moment sparkle and shine,
No matter what was going on, everything would be fine.

Things that I celebrate in July

www.ingramcontent.com/pod-product-compliance
Lightning Source LLC
Chambersburg PA
CBHW041714160426
43209CB00018B/1832